Tails of Wisdom

Leadership, Love, & Life Lessons from My Feline Overlords

Rashmie Joy

Copyright © <Published Year> <Author Name>

Made with ❤ on the Notion Press Platform

www.notionpress.com

Contents

Chapter 1: Welcome to the Feline Academy of Life

"The greatest teachers don't stand at the front of a classroom.

Sometimes, they sit at your back door, waiting to be fed."

If you're looking for a book grounded in logic, carefully structured theories, and well-researched life strategies—this isn't it. In fact, I highly recommend tossing logic out the window before you continue reading. Life isn't always logical, and neither are cats. And yet, these fluffy, moody, and often unpredictable creatures seem to have mastered what most of us spend a lifetime trying to figure out—how to live unapologetically.

Over the years, I've had the privilege (or misfortune, depending on the day) of being surrounded by a band of feline overlords—each with their own quirks, boundaries, and social hierarchies. What started as simply feeding a few stray cats at my back door quickly turned into an accidental mentorship program, where I— a supposedly rational human—became the student.

My feline professors, through their daily antics, fights, betrayals, love affairs, and occasional food-related wars, have taught me more about leadership, relationships, boundaries, and emotional intelligence than any self-help book ever could.

Why Cats Make the Ultimate Teachers

Let's be honest—cats don't need us. They tolerate us, they use us for food and warmth, and when they grace us with their affection, it's entirely on their terms. And therein lies their first lesson: self-respect and boundaries. Cats don't people-please. They don't waste time doubting their worth. They walk through life with an unshakable sense of entitlement, as if the entire universe exists for their convenience. Imagine if we could all move through life with that level of confidence and clarity!

Unlike humans, who constantly struggle with social expectations, self-doubt, and the need for external validation, cats exist in a state of absolute certainty. If they don't like you, you'll know. If they do like you, they might let you pet them—if you're lucky. They don't explain their choices, they don't justify their needs, and they certainly don't apologize for their moods. And yet, despite their independence, they have a remarkable ability to forge deep bonds to express love in their own way, and to demand respect in every interaction.

The Origins of My Cat Squad

I have always been a cat person. I wished for a cat for years, but life always made it seem impossible. Yet, in ways I couldn't predict, the Universe had already set things in motion. Before GG, before Batman, before the entire Cat Squad, there were small moments—foreshadowings—that hinted at the feline-filled future waiting for me.

It all began with **GG** the kitten—a tiny, meowing ball of fluff who walked into our lives one evening, crying from under the bike. My first instinct was to offer her a bowl of diluted milk, and just like that, the Cat Squad was born.

Next came **Batman** and **Vivian**. Batman, the sleek black ruler of the backyard, established his presence with quiet authority, while Vivian, cautious and reserved, kept her distance until trust was earned. What started with three quickly grew into a full-fledged feline monarchy—complete with love stories, feuds, shifting alliances, and the occasional coup d'état over food bowls.

Throw in **Daisy**, the Ice Queen; **Maple**, the unbothered philosopher; **Chairman Mao**, the talkative dictator; **Casper**, the overzealous canine bodyguard, and I suddenly found myself at the centre of a furry soap opera. But the saga doesn't end there.

Then came **Smokey**, the rival tom, constantly challenging Batman's authority—a feline power struggle worth its own chapter. **Mittens**, the occasional visitor, cautious yet determined to claim her safe space. And finally, **Ginger**, the mysterious orange cat who appeared out of nowhere, radiating an almost mystical presence.

And let's not forget the two unexpected supporting characters—**my daughter**, the consummate partner-in-crime, and **the husband**, the former cat sceptics turned fierce protector (who, on multiple occasions, has ranted about eradicating dogs from the planet while standing guard with a jug of water to defend the cats).

From territorial disputes to food diplomacy, from unspoken alliances to unexpected betrayals, these cats have turned my home into a masterclass in leadership, trust, and human (or feline) dynamics. And while my hands have endured a fair share of bites and scratches, my mind has been opened to a whole new way of navigating life's challenges.

What This Book is Really About

This isn't just a book about cats. It's about life, leadership, love, and boundaries—told through the eyes (and claws) of the best teachers I've ever had. You'll find humour, you'll find wisdom, and most importantly, you'll find practical takeaways that you can apply to your own relationships, workplace, and personal growth.

Each chapter explores a key lesson inspired by my feline overlords, blending light-hearted storytelling with deeper reflections on what it truly means to lead, love, and live without apology. Whether it's Batman's quiet authority, Daisy's unwavering boundaries, Chairman Mao's strategic communication, or Casper's overzealous loyalty, there's something to be learned from each of them.

But before the Cat Squad took over my life, there were moments—small, seemingly unrelated incidents—that hinted at what was to come. In hindsight, they weren't coincidences. They were signs. And so, before we dive into the lessons from my feline overlords, let's start at the very beginning—with the first whispers of a cat-filled destiny.

So, as you turn the pages, read with an open mind, embrace the absurdity, and prepare to take notes—because these cats have a lot to teach.

And if you happen to have a cat staring at you as you read this, congratulations. You've already been chosen as a student.

Welcome to the Feline Academy of Life!

Meet the Overlords (and Their Loyal Staff)

Because you deserve to know who really runs the show around here.

The Cats:

GG (AKA Grey Goose)

The OG of the Cat Squad — tiny, fierce, and the reason this madness

began. Taught everyone how to set boundaries without lifting a paw.

Batman

All-black, all-business. The quiet king who rules with a stare. Doesn't

start fights — just finishes them by existing.

Vivian

The drama queen in velvet fur. Might've been royalty in a past life.

Poised, and perpetually three steps ahead of everyone.

Daisy

Soft-spoken? Nope. Soft-footed stalker with trust issues and killer side-

eye. Thinks you're sketchy, even while eating the food served by you.

Maple

Pretty, pouty, and passive aggressive. Uses humans as shields. Will scream like a banshee, then act like nothing happened.

Chairman Mao

A loud revolutionary in a small, furry body. Meows like it's a political statement. Bit the hand that fed her — then apologized by snuggling it.

Smokey

The muscle. Always looks like he's about to challenge someone to a duel. Doesn't believe in personal space, unless it's his own.

Mittens

The sweet ninja. Appears, eats, disappears. Zero drama.

Cautious but loyal — once she trusts you, you're in for life.

Ginger

The cosmic visitor. Mysterious, aloof, might be from another timeline.

Shows up when you least expect him... or need a spiritual awakening. (I

haven't been able to get a picture of him!)

The Dog

Casper

The bodyguard who appointed himself. Loyal, dramatic, confused.

Protects me like I'm a celebrity — and he's head of PR.

The Humans

Me (The Author)

Accidental cat matriarch. Didn't ask for a feline empire — inherited one anyway. Still unsure if I'm training them or being trained.

My Daughter

Partner in crime and food distribution. Wields a stick like a seasoned ninja. Understands every cat's vibe without speaking a word.

The Husband

Former cat sceptics, now full-time Cat Security Chief.

Carries a jug of water to douse other stray dogs like it's a sacred weapon — which, frankly, it is.

Chapter 2: Ask and You Shall Receive & Foreshadowing

"The Universe listens—not always in the way we expect, but in the way we need. Pay attention to the signs, no matter how small."

I have always been a cat person. Even before I had cats, I knew in my heart that one day, I would have one as a pet. But at the same time, I was realistic. I understood the time, space, and commitment it takes to be a pet parent, and I wasn't sure how it would ever happen. Still, I never stopped hoping, wishing, and quietly manifesting the idea of having a cat in my life.

What I have since learned is this: when you truly, deeply desire something, the Universe has a way of presenting you with tiny opportunities—little tests to see if you're ready.

If you recognize them and show up, you provide the Universe with evidence that you're prepared. And when you prove you're ready, the Universe delivers in ways you never could have predicted.

Looking back, there were two completely unrelated incidents that foreshadowed just how entangled my life would become with cats.

Incident 1: The Husband vs. The Terrace Intruder

One day, The Husband went up to the terrace and left the door open by mistake. Lo and behold, a mystery cat snuck in. Not just anywhere—she sat patiently on the stairs, waiting.

Now, let's be clear: at this point in time, The Husband was not a fan of cats. So when he realized a feline had made herself at home, his reaction was pure panic.

Instead of simply walking past her, he went into full crisis mode—wiggling his way around her, retreating down the stairs, and frantically calling me for backup.

I had no idea what the ruckus was about. When I got upstairs, I was greeted by a calm, composed cat who was definitely not in a hurry to leave. Unlike The Husband, I approached her with gentle words and open energy. Within moments, she gracefully exited. No drama, no panic—just an unspoken understanding between two creatures who respected each other's space.

Looking back, it feels like the first test. A moment that hinted at what was to come.

Incident 2: The Unexpected Arrival of Vivian

Fast forward to 2023. Our house was undergoing major renovations. The doors were wide open, and anyone—or anything—could sneak in. And one did. Enter Vivian.

She was just a tiny kitten back then, but she had full access to the entire house. I would find her in the most unexpected places—a quiet observer, never too far away but never too close.

I started leaving food and water on the terrace for her, but my attempts to get near her were unsuccessful. She was watching, waiting—perhaps deciding whether I was worthy of her trust.

Meanwhile, The Husband was not pleased.

- He frequently muttered under his breath about how the house was "not a jungle."

- He threw around dramatic accusations, including blaming Vivian for "murdering" a pigeon almost her size. (To this day, there's no evidence.)

- He was convinced that this was temporary. (Spoiler: It wasn't.)

Vivian had arrived, and she was here to stay.

Ask, and You Shall Receive—But Be Ready for the Unexpected

I spent years wishing for a cat. And the Universe responded—not by handing me a single pet cat in a neat little package, but by presenting me with opportunities to step up. First, a cat on the terrace to see how I'd react. Then, a tiny kitten who claimed our space before we could even question it.

And now? I have nine cats and a dog, and my life is completely intertwined with them. I never could have imagined it unfolding this way. But that's the beauty of the Universe—it delivers in ways that are far better, wilder, and more meaningful than we ever plan for.

When you truly want something, don't stress over the "how" or "when." The Universe is already working on it.

Recognize small opportunities—they are your signposts. How you respond to the small things determines whether you're ready for the big things.

Trust that things will unfold in the best way for you. Maybe not how you imagined—but always how you need them to.

Looking back, I laugh at how much The Husband resisted in the beginning. And now? He's the one reminding me when the cat food is running low.

So be careful what you ask for—because the Universe is always

listening. And sometimes, it answers with nine cats and a dog.

Chapter 3: Kings & Challengers— The Power Struggle

"Power isn't about who growls the loudest—it's about who can command respect without ever raising a paw."

If there's one thing cats don't do, it's share power easily. And when two strong personalities collide, the result is a never-ending battle for dominance, territory, and respect. Enter Batman, the established ruler of the back door, and Smokey, the challenger determined to shake things up.

Unlike some rivalries that fizzle out, this one has endured. It is a game of strategy, psychology, and sometimes, full-on combat. But as I've observed their battles, I've realized that what looks like pure animal instinct is actually a lesson in leadership, identity, and the different ways power can be claimed.

Batman: The Silent Ruler

Batman was king of the back door long before Smokey arrived. He didn't seize power—he simply became power. He didn't need to fight for respect because it was already understood. His leadership is quiet, stable, and unquestioned—until Smokey walked in.

He rules through presence, not aggression. Batman doesn't need to flex his authority—he simply exists with confidence, and the others follow.

He picks his battles wisely. He doesn't engage in needless fights, but when he does, it's swift, decisive, and effective.

He values order and consistency. His leadership style is built on keeping things running smoothly, with minimal disruption.

For a long time, this worked. And then Smokey appeared.

Smokey: The Challenger

Smokey didn't tiptoe in cautiously. He stormed in like a rebel with something to prove. A muscular tom with the energy of a cat who has fought (and won) many battles, he was clearly not here to take orders.

He challenges authority at every turn. He doesn't care about tradition—if there's power to be had, he wants it.

He believes leadership must be constantly reinforced. Unlike Batman, who holds authority effortlessly, Smokey is convinced that control must be displayed, fought for, and maintained.

He has no patience for silent dominance. If you're in charge, he wants to see proof—daily.

Their fundamental differences mean that their paths were always going to collide.

The Stages of Their Rivalry

Their battles are predictable, following a script that both of them understand but refuse to deviate from:

1.The Stand-Off: They see each other. They stop. The air gets heavy. There is no movement—just two figures locked in an unspoken challenge.

2.The Growl-Hiss Exchange: Smokey is usually the first to escalate. Low growls, deep stares, tails puffed up. Batman responds, but only if necessary.

3.The Physical Clash: If neither backs down, fur flies. A blur of claws, rolled-up bodies, and a flurry of kicks ensue. It's fast, brutal, and over within seconds.

4.The Aftermath: No matter how intense the fight, they always walk away in one piece. Their battles are about principle, not destruction.

This cycle has repeated itself countless times, and yet, neither cat has fully claimed victory.

The Psychology Behind the Power Struggle

Their battle isn't just about food or space—it's a classic leadership struggle. Two different approaches, two different philosophies:

- **Batman believes in silent authority, respect through consistency, and ruling without unnecessary aggression.**

- **Smokey believes in physical dominance, visible control, and proving power through repeated displays of force.**

It's a real-world leadership dynamic we see everywhere: Some lead by quiet influence, others lead by constant assertion.

Their fights have taught me that leadership is not about being the loudest or strongest—it's about knowing when to act and when to stand firm.

Final Thoughts: An Unfinished War

Their rivalry is far from over. Some days are peaceful, others are tense with impending confrontation. But one thing is certain: neither Batman nor Smokey is backing down.

And maybe, that's exactly how it's meant to be. Two kings, locked in an eternal battle, both shaping and defining what true leadership means in the feline world.

Chapter 4: Leadership Lessons from the Cat Kingdom

"A true leader knows when to step forward, when to step back, and when to simply observe."

If there's one thing cats understand better than humans, it's how to command respect without demanding it. They don't chase approval. They don't explain themselves. And yet, they walk into a room with the kind of authority that CEOs and world leaders could only dream of.

As someone who has spent years managing teams, coaching leaders, and navigating human dynamics, I've come to realize that cats have mastered leadership in ways that humans struggle with. In the feline world, leadership isn't about control—it's about presence, influence, and the fine art of knowing when to act and when to simply exist in silent power.

In this chapter, we explore the three great leaders of the Cat Kingdom—each with a unique leadership style. From the regal authority of Batman to the vocal influence of Chairman Mao, to the overzealous security policies of Casper, these feline and canine leaders offer hilarious yet profound insights into effective leadership.

The Art of the Royal Saunter – Leadership Lessons from Batman

Batman was never elected leader of the Cat Squad—he just became one. He didn't fight for it, didn't campaign for it, and certainly didn't ask for permission. He simply carried himself like a king, and the rest followed.

What makes Batman such an effective leader?

He commands without controlling. He never chases the others around. Instead, they move when he moves, adjust when he adjusts. True leaders don't micromanage—they inspire movement through presence.

He picks his battles wisely. Unlike some cats (looking at you, Daisy), Batman doesn't engage in needless conflict. But when his authority is questioned, he makes one decisive move — a stare, a well-timed swat, or a dignified exit that reminds everyone who the real boss is.

He understands the power of patience. Batman doesn't react impulsively. He watches, calculates, and only steps in when absolutely necessary. In leadership, patience and observation are often more powerful than action.

Human Leadership Takeaway: Confidence and quiet authority can be more effective than loud commands. Own your space, lead with presence, and pick your battles wisely.

Chairman Mao: The Power of Vocal Leadership

Chairman Mao (who, as it turns out, is actually a Chairwoman) has a very different leadership style. While Batman relies on silent authority, Chairman Mao leads through communication. She meows in greeting, meows while eating, meows when she wants attention, and meows in protest if she doesn't get it. Her voice is her power.

How does Chairman Mao's vocal leadership translate into human wisdom?

She ensures she's heard. Chairman Mao makes sure her presence is known—not through force, but through consistent, strategic communication. Leaders who articulate their vision clearly and regularly are the ones who gain influence.

She builds relationships through engagement. Unlike Batman, who leads through distance, Chairman Mao thrives on interaction. She is always present, engaging, and making sure her needs (and the needs of the squad) are known.

She uses emotion to drive action. If she needs food, attention, or a warm lap, she makes sure her message is emotionally compelling. Effective leaders understand that logic alone doesn't drive action—emotional connection does.

Human Leadership Takeaway: Communication is key. Speak up, engage with your team, and use the power of consistent messaging to lead effectively.

Casper's Security Firm: The Dangers of Overprotective Leadership

And then there's Casper. If Batman is the composed ruler and Chairman Mao is the charismatic diplomat, then Casper is the head of security who takes his job way too seriously.

Casper believes it is his divine duty to follow me everywhere. Every time I step outside, he materializes like an overzealous bodyguard, convinced that I need protection from absolutely nothing. He is determined, loyal, and completely oblivious to personal space.

He confuses control with care. Casper's heart is in the right place, but his constant hovering and interference create unnecessary chaos. Leaders who micromanage often think they're being helpful, but in reality, they're suffocating their team.

He disrupts more than he protects. Casper's idea of 'security' sometimes causes more problems than solutions—like when he stands right in the middle of feeding time, sending the cats into a panic. Leaders who overstep their role often create resistance instead of trust.

He's lovable—but exhausting. Everyone adores Casper, but sometimes, you just need a moment without supervision. Even well-intentioned leaders need to give people (or cats) room to breathe.

Human Leadership Takeaway: Protect, but don't suffocate. Great leaders empower others by offering guidance—not by standing over their shoulders.

Final Thoughts: Lessons from the Cat Kingdom

Leadership isn't about being the loudest, the most controlling, or even the most charismatic. The Cat Squad teaches us that great leadership can take many forms:

- **Batman's silent authority reminds us that confidence and presence are more powerful than force.**

- **Chairman Mao's vocal leadership shows the importance of communication and engagement.**

- **Casper's overprotectiveness highlights the dangers of micromanagement and the importance of trust.**

Whether you're leading a company, a team, or just trying to manage your own life better—there's something to be learned from the Cat Kingdom. And if you ever need a leadership coach, just find a cat and observe. They've got it all figured out.

Chapter 5: Mittens and The Art of Cautious Trust

"Not all trust looks the same. Some connections are built on slow, steady steps rather than leaps of faith."

Not all cats seek attention. Some observe from the sidelines, assessing, waiting, and deciding if and when they'll engage. And then there's Mittens—the cat who walks the fine line between belonging and staying distant.

She isn't a regular like Batman, Daisy, or Chairman Mao. She isn't a complete outsider either. She is the in-betweener—the visitor who stays just out of reach.

Mittens has perfected the art of being present without fully committing. She watches from the shadows, appearing just long enough to take what she needs and then slipping away before anyone can get too close.

She waits for absolute safety before approaching. No sudden movements. No unnecessary risks. She only comes forward when she's 100% sure she won't be disturbed.

She takes what's given but never asks for more. Unlike Chairman Mao, who demands attention loudly, Mittens accepts what's available but never insists.

She trusts—at a distance. She knows she's welcome, but she doesn't push the limits of that welcome. She remains independent yet connected.

In a way, Mittens represents the kind of people who prefer to stay on the periphery—watching, absorbing, and engaging on their own terms.

Why Some Relationships Stay at Arm's Length

Mittens reminds me that not every relationship needs to be intense or all-consuming. Some connections are meant to exist at a comfortable distance.

Not everyone wants deep attachment. Some people (and cats) thrive best when they have space. It's not about rejection—it's about personal boundaries.

Trust is a personal journey. While other cats throw themselves into the mix, Mittens takes her time, building trust slowly. She is proof that trust doesn't have to look the same for everyone.

Presence is enough. Even if she never fully joins the squad, her presence alone has an impact. Sometimes, being there—even from a distance—is meaningful enough.

Final Thoughts: The Wisdom of Mittens

Mittens may never become a full-fledged member of the Cat Squad, and that's okay. She doesn't need to be. She exists in the space between, and that's where she is comfortable.

- **She reminds us that connection doesn't have to be constant to be real.**

- **She shows that trust has many forms—and all of them are valid.**

- **She teaches us that belonging is a choice, not an obligation.**

Some visitors stay. Others drift in and out of our lives. Either way, their presence still matters.

Chapter 6: Boundaries & Self-Respect—Hissing is Healthy

"The strongest boundaries don't need to be shouted. A quiet, unwavering

'no' is just as powerful."

If there's one thing cats do better than anyone, it's setting boundaries. They don't over-explain, feel guilty, or negotiate their needs. If they don't want attention, they walk away. If they don't like being touched, they make it very clear (sometimes with claws). And if they feel their space is invaded—well, let's just say the offender won't make that mistake twice.

Meanwhile, humans struggle to say "no" without feeling guilty. We tolerate discomfort, let people push our limits, and often explain ourselves when we really shouldn't have to. But the Cat Kingdom? It operates by one simple rule: If you don't respect my boundary, you will suffer the consequences.

In this chapter, we explore the feline masters of boundary-setting, each with their own style. From Daisy's no-nonsense approach, to Chairman Mao's bite-first-ask-questions-later policy, to GG's quiet but firm signals, we'll learn what it really means to stand your ground without apology.

Daisy's Zero-Tolerance Policy: The Power of Boundaries

Daisy has zero patience for nonsense. While some cats may tolerate unwanted attention before snapping, Daisy skips the warning phase entirely. If another cat gets too close, she hisses, growls, and—if necessary—launches into a full-on attack. Humans? No exceptions. She may accept the food, but personal space is non-negotiable.

Her message is simple: Respect my space or prepare for battle.

She doesn't waste energy on politeness. Daisy doesn't smile through discomfort or suffer fools. If she's not interested, she makes it known—immediately.

She doesn't explain her boundaries. You'll never see Daisy justifying why she hissed at you. She doesn't need your approval to set limits.

She enforces her boundaries consistently. No exceptions, no blurred lines. The first offense is also the last.

Human Boundary Takeaway: Stop over-explaining your boundaries. No is a complete sentence.

When Love Bites – Chairman Mao's Unexpected Feedback

Chairman Mao loves affection. She's clingy, vocal, and enjoys being petted. Until she doesn't.

One moment, she's purring under my hands—content and happy. The next, she's sinking her teeth into my hand as if I've committed an unforgivable offense.

What did I do? No idea. Maybe I touched a sore spot. Maybe she suddenly remembered something offensive I did weeks ago. Maybe she's a cat being a cat. Or maybe, like many of us, she simply hit her social limit and snapped.

She teaches us that boundaries can change in real-time. What was okay a minute ago might not be okay now—and that's valid.

She doesn't let guilt override her needs. There's no internal debate. If she needs space, she takes it. No second-guessing.

She gives instant feedback. Unlike humans, who let resentment fester, Chairman Mao addresses the issue immediately. (Even if that 'feedback' comes in the form of teeth.)

Human Boundary Takeaway: If something feels wrong, you don't have to tolerate it just because you tolerated it before.

Batman the Casanova: How to Handle Rejection Like a Pro

Batman considers himself a ladies' man. He struts around serenading all the female cats—Daisy, Maple, Vivian, Chairman Mao. The response? Slaps. Many slaps.

Chairman Mao gives him a swift and brutal rejection. Maple tolerates him until she doesn't. Daisy, the Boundary Queen, goes for a theatrical double slap with sound effects.

Does that discourage him? Not at all. Batman doesn't sulk, get offended, or question his self-worth. He simply backs off, regroups, and tries again later.

He doesn't take rejection personally. It's not about him—it's about their boundaries. And he respects that.

He doesn't beg for attention. If it's not reciprocated, he moves on. No whining, no self-pity.

He knows persistence has limits. When he realizes a no is a hard no, he doesn't push. He walks away with dignity.

Human Boundary Takeaway: Rejection isn't a personal attack.

Respect the no, adjust, and move on gracefully.

GG's Subtle Boundaries: The Quiet Enforcer

GG was never aggressive. She never hissed, growled, or lashed out. But she was a master of silent boundaries.

If she didn't want to be touched, she would simply move away. No drama, no conflict—just a firm, quiet decision. If another cat tried to take her food, she wouldn't fight. She'd simply sit on it, making it clear that this meal was hers.

Her approach was subtle but undeniable. And everyone respected it.

She made her boundaries clear without aggression. No need for violence—just quiet confidence.

She didn't reward bad behavior. If another cat pushed too much, she left. She didn't stick around trying to "fix" the situation.

She stayed firm without being confrontational. She didn't react emotionally—she just reinforced her limits calmly.

Human Boundary Takeaway: You don't have to be loud or aggressive to set boundaries. You just have to be consistent.

Final Thoughts: What the Cats Teach Us About Boundaries

Cats don't waste time explaining, justifying, or second-guessing their boundaries. They simply enforce them. Whether it's through a hiss, a bite, a slap, or a quiet exit, they set limits and expect them to be respected.

- **Daisy reminds us that a strong no needs no explanation.**

- **Chairman Mao shows us that boundaries can change, and that's okay.**

- **Batman proves that rejection isn't a personal attack.**

- **GG teaches us that quiet, firm boundaries are just as powerful.**

In a world where people constantly push limits, be like a cat. Set boundaries, enforce them without guilt, and remember—hissing is healthy.

Chapter 7: Relationships—Navigating Love, Trust & Social Hierarchies

"Love and trust aren't about control—they're about understanding when to stay close and when to give space."

Cats are masters of relationships. They form alliances, enforce hierarchies, and establish trust—on their own terms. Unlike humans, who overcomplicate things with mixed signals, unspoken expectations, and unnecessary drama, cats operate with clarity and precision. If they like you, they'll show it. If they don't, they'll also show it (sometimes with claws).

Relationships—whether between humans or cats—are built on trust, communication, and understanding personal boundaries. And just like in any social circle, there are moments of loyalty, betrayal, unexpected alliances, and the occasional battle over food.

In this chapter, we dive into the complex dynamics of feline relationships—from Vivian's slow-burn trust-building to the great food preference mystery, to Maple's survival-driven relationship tactics. Each offers an unexpected but insightful lesson on navigating love, trust, and social interactions.

Vivian's Trust Blueprint: Why Relationships Take Time

Vivian is the epitome of caution. She's spent months observing from a distance, carefully analyzing human-cat interactions before making a single move. Unlike some cats (looking at you, Chairman Mao), she doesn't rush into relationships. Instead, she operates on a principle that most humans should adopt: Trust is earned, not freely given.

She observes before engaging. Vivian spent seven months watching before deciding it was safe to approach. She teaches us that rushing into relationships—whether friendships or partnerships—without understanding the dynamics first can lead to regret.

She tests before trusting. First, she accepted food. Then, she tolerated proximity. Only after a long probation period did she allow physical contact. Humans, take notes—relationships built on gradual trust last longer than those formed in haste.

She never fully lets her guard down. Even after establishing trust, Vivian still remains observant. She teaches us that trust doesn't mean blind faith—it means choosing to engage with awareness.

Human Relationship Takeaway: Trust should be built step by step. Observe, engage cautiously, and remember that real trust takes time.

The Great Food Swap Mystery: Love & Understanding Differences

Some relationships are built on common values. Others are built on sheer confusion. Case in point: Chairman Mao prefers dog food, and Casper prefers cat food.

No explanation. No logic. Just a complete rejection of their own species' diets.

This baffling dynamic raises an important question—why do we assume that people (or animals) will naturally like what they're "supposed to" like?

Not everyone wants what's expected of them. Just like Chairman Mao rejected cat food, people often reject traditional expectations. Careers, relationships, and lifestyles don't have to follow a predefined formula.

What works for one may not work for another. Casper loves cat food. Chairman Mao loves dog food. Neither is wrong—it's just personal preference. The same applies to human relationships—different people thrive under different conditions.

Compatibility isn't about sameness—it's about respect. Despite their opposite food preferences, Casper and Chairman Mao coexist peacefully. The best relationships aren't always between identical people, but between those who accept each other's differences.

Human Relationship Takeaway: People (and cats) don't always fit into predefined molds. True connection is about respecting differences, not forcing conformity.

Casualties of Love: When a Cat Uses You as a Human Shield

Enter Maple, the master strategist. Unlike Vivian, who builds trust carefully, or Chairman Mao, who demands attention, Maple uses tactical alliances to navigate tricky situations.

During feeding time, if Casper (the overenthusiastic bodyguard) is near, Maple makes a strategic move:

→ She presses herself against my leg and yowls dramatically. → She ensures that I, the human, stand between her and Casper. → She eats in peace, using me as a literal shield.

While this is highly amusing (and slightly manipulative), Maple teaches an important

relationship lesson: People (and cats) sometimes leverage relationships for safety.

Some relationships are about protection. Maple doesn't seek affection from me—she seeks security. Some relationships, especially in difficult circumstances, are about having someone to stand between you and the chaos.

Strategic alliances have value. Maple may not be my most affectionate cat, but she knows the importance of aligning with the right person at the right time. In workplaces, friendships, and partnerships, alliances can be just as valuable as deep bonds.

Not all relationships are meant to be deeply emotional. Some are built on mutual benefit—and that's okay. Not every relationship needs to be about deep connection; some are about navigating the world more safely.

Human Relationship Takeaway: Recognize the different roles people play in your life. Some offer emotional depth, some offer protection, and some simply help you survive the moment.

Final Thoughts: Lessons in Love, Trust & Social Dynamics

Relationships—whether feline or human—are about trust, respect, and understanding personal needs. Cats may seem detached, but they actually form deep, meaningful connections based on trust and mutual benefit.

- **Vivian reminds us that trust is earned, not given freely.**

- **Chairman Mao and Casper show us that compatibility isn't about being the same—it's about respect.**

- **Maple teaches us that relationships come in different forms, and not all are built on emotion—some are strategic.**

In a world full of complicated human relationships, sometimes, the best teachers have fur, whiskers, and a slightly condescending stare.

So, the next time you find yourself overthinking relationships, ask yourself—what would a cat do?

Answer: Set boundaries, demand food, and walk away when necessary.

Chapter 8: Mindfulness & The Art of Being Unbothered

"A cat doesn't stress about tomorrow. It stretches in the sun, sleeps when it's tired, and lives fully in the moment. So should we."

If there's one thing cats have mastered, it's the fine art of being unbothered. They don't waste time overthinking, worrying about the future, or regretting the past. They exist completely in the present moment—whether it's basking in a sunbeam, watching a bird with laser focus, or knocking an object off a table just to see what happens.

Meanwhile, humans overthink, stress about things beyond their control, and dwell on what-ifs that will never happen. Cats? They live with graceful detachment—fully engaged in life, yet never burdened by it.

In this chapter, we explore the feline masters of mindfulness—from Maple's effortless calm, to Daisy's selective attention, to Batman's ability to conserve energy like a Zen monk.

Maple's Meditation Method: How to Stay Unbothered in Chaos

Maple is the epitome of calm. While other cats react with dramatic flair, Maple simply exists. If another cat hisses at her, she doesn't engage. If Casper rushes too close, she takes a few steps back— not out of fear, but because she can't be bothered.

She doesn't absorb other cats' emotions. If someone is having a meltdown, that's their problem. Maple stays detached.

She moves through life effortlessly. She explores, observes, but never overreacts. Her energy is reserved for things that actually matter.

She finds peace in simple moments. Whether it's staring at a wall (what does she see?!), stretching in a sunbeam, or sitting quietly while the world spins around her—she teaches us that stillness is powerful.

Human Mindfulness Takeaway: You don't have to engage in every conflict. Choose where your energy goes, and don't let external chaos disturb your peace.

Daisy & Selective Awareness: The Art of Ignoring What Doesn't Serve You

Daisy is hyper-aware of everything—except for things she deems unimportant. Unlike Maple, who radiates Zen energy,

Daisy is strategically selective about where she focuses her attention. She chooses what deserves her time and energy.

She doesn't react to every stimulus. Loud noise? She doesn't flinch. Someone trying to pet her without permission? She walks away. Not everything requires a response.

She knows when to engage and when to disengage. She watches, calculates, and then decides—is this worth my time? If not, she moves on.

She doesn't give energy to things she can't control. Dogs barking? Humans being annoying? Not her problem. She teaches us that we waste too much energy worrying about things outside our control.

Human Mindfulness Takeaway: Not everything deserves your reaction. Ignore what doesn't serve you and engage only when it's worth it.

Batman's Energy Conservation Philosophy: Work Smarter, Not Harder

Batman is a master strategist. Unlike hyperactive cats that chase every little thing, Batman moves only when necessary. He spends most of his time lounging, waiting, and watching—because he understands that energy is a precious resource.

He never rushes. While other cats panic or overreact, Batman takes his time. He doesn't waste energy on unnecessary movement.

He knows that presence is more powerful than action. He doesn't need to prove himself with constant effort—his mere presence commands respect.

He understands the value of rest. While humans glorify hustle culture, Batman teaches us that resting is productive. Energy must be preserved and used wisely.

Human Mindfulness Takeaway: Stop glorifying busyness. Slow down, observe, and use your energy intentionally.

Final Thoughts: The Feline Guide to Mindful Living

If mindfulness had a mascot, it would be a cat basking in the sun. They exist fully in the present, detached from unnecessary stress, and completely at ease with themselves.

- **Maple reminds us to stay calm and disengage from unnecessary drama.**

- **Daisy teaches us that not everything deserves our attention.**

- **Batman shows us that energy is a resource—use it wisely.**

In a world that demands urgency and overreaction, be like a cat. Slow down, choose peace, and stop wasting energy on things that don't matter.

Chapter 9: Ginger—The Mysterious Wanderer

"Not all who enter our lives are meant to stay. Some are messengers,

here to whisper wisdom before they disappear."

Some cats arrive with a presence so fleeting, so enigmatic, that they feel less like visitors and more like whispers of something unseen. Ginger is one such cat. He comes and goes as he pleases, appearing without warning, disappearing just as suddenly. A flash of orange fur, a glint of knowing eyes, and then—he's gone.

While the rest of the Cat Squad has settled into a rhythm, Ginger remains a mystery. He isn't a regular, yet he isn't a stranger. He exists on the edges, belonging to no one and nowhere, yet leaving an undeniable impression wherever he appears.

The Presence of the Unseen

Ginger's rare appearances feel almost deliberate. It's as if he chooses his moments, stepping into the scene like an observer, never staying long enough to be fully known.

He never stays in one place. While the other cats have territories, favourite sunbathing spots, and familiar paths, Ginger doesn't. He is untethered, free, and impossible to predict.

He isn't bound by routine. There is no set time for his visits. He may show up three days in a row, then vanish for weeks, as if drawn by some invisible force that only he understands.

He is always watching. Even when he isn't seen, I suspect he's near. There's an awareness in his gaze—a quiet acknowledgment that he sees far more than he reveals.

His presence is not just physical—it's an energy.

The Symbolism of the Drifter

Some beings aren't meant to stay. They come into our

lives to leave a mark, not a permanent presence. Ginger reminds me of

the people who enter briefly but change something fundamental within

us.

Not all connections require permanence. Some of the most meaningful

encounters are the ones that last only a moment. It doesn't make them

any less significant.

Freedom and belonging aren't opposites. Ginger belongs everywhere

and nowhere at once. He is both part of the world and apart from it.

Mystery has its own kind of wisdom. While we crave understanding, sometimes the greatest lessons come from what we cannot fully explain.

The Universe is constantly communicating with us. It teaches through people, nature, and even the most fleeting interactions. We just need to keep our eyes, ears, and—more importantly—our minds and hearts open.

Final Thoughts: The Wisdom of the Phantom Wanderer

Ginger may never become a full-time resident of the Cat Squad. He may always remain on the fringes, stepping in only when he chooses. But that doesn't make his presence any less real.

- **He reminds us that not all who wander are lost.**

- **He teaches that meaningful encounters don't require permanence.**

- **He shows that presence can be felt—even in absence.**

- **And above all, he reminds us to listen—to the Universe, to nature, and to the quiet wisdom in things we don't fully understand.**

Some connections defy logic. Some beings exist beyond our understanding. And some, like Ginger, leave behind a feeling rather than a footprint.

Chapter 10: Letting Go—Loss, Love & Acceptance

"Grief is not about forgetting—it's about remembering with love instead of pain."

Loss is one of the hardest lessons life teaches us. Whether it's the passing of a beloved pet, the end of a relationship, or a chapter of life closing, letting go forces us to confront our deepest emotions. And yet, if there's one thing that cats have shown me, it's that loss—while painful—is also an inevitable part of life's cycle.

Cats don't cling. They don't dwell on what was. They adapt, move forward, and continue to exist in the present moment. But as humans, we struggle with this. We hold on too tightly, afraid that letting go means losing what we love.

This chapter is dedicated to GG, the tiny kitten who started it all, and the lessons she left behind.

Saying Goodbye to GG—Love

That Lives Beyond Loss

GG was the first. The tiny meows that called from beneath the bike that evening marked the beginning of the Cat Squad. She walked into our lives, accepted the milk we offered, and in her short time with us, she became an integral part of our family.

And then, one night, she was gone. Attacked by dogs, injured beyond saving, she left before I could do anything to stop it. I held her as she took her last breaths, and in that moment, I realized just how deeply we can love something—even when we know we can't keep it forever.

Her loss hurt in ways I hadn't expected. She was tiny, fragile, innocent— and gone too soon. But what GG taught me, even in her absence, is that love doesn't disappear with loss. It lingers in the memories, in the lessons, in the way she changed my heart.

Love is never wasted. Even if it doesn't last as long as we want, the love we give and receive leaves an imprint that never fades.

Letting go isn't forgetting. Moving forward doesn't mean erasing the past—it means carrying it differently.

Grief is a teacher. It forces us to sit with emotions we'd rather avoid. But in doing so, it reshapes us, softens us, and reminds us what truly matters.

Human Takeaway: Love fully, even knowing it's temporary. The pain of loss is the price of deep connection, and it's always worth it.

The Cycle of Life—Watching the Cat Squad Grow & Change

Life has a way of continuing, even when we feel like it shouldn't. The day after GG's passing, the other cats still had to be fed. The sun still rose. The world moved forward, even though my heart felt like it had stopped.

Over time, more cats came. Batman, Vivian, Daisy, Maple, Chairman Mao, and eventually, even Casper. And most recently, new kittens—Daisy's and Vivian's—have found their way into the world, carrying on the cycle of life.

Watching them, I realized something profound: Life doesn't wait for us to be ready. It just keeps unfolding.

Loss creates space for new beginnings. One chapter ends, another begins—whether we're ready or not.

Holding on too tightly keeps us stuck. The more we resist change, the harder it is to move forward.

Life moves at its own pace. And sometimes, all we can do is surrender to its rhythm.

Human Takeaway: Loss isn't the end—it's part of the journey. Even in grief, life finds a way to keep going, and so must we.

When Attachments Hurt—Learning to Love Without Clinging

Cats have an incredible ability to love without attachment. They form bonds, but they don't hold on desperately. If something changes, they adapt. Humans, on the other hand, struggle with this.

We cling. We resist change. We fear letting go because we think it means losing something permanently. But love—real love—isn't about possession. It's about presence.

Cats love freely, not fearfully. They don't spend time worrying about what happens next. They just exist in the now.

Love isn't about control. It's about trusting that what's meant to stay will stay, and what's meant to go will go.

Sometimes, the best way to love is to let go. Holding on too tightly can suffocate what we're trying to keep.

Human Takeaway: Love fully, but don't fear change. True love is about presence, not possession.

Final Thoughts: What the Cats Teach Us About Letting Go

Cats don't hold grudges, dwell on the past, or resist the flow of life. They accept what is, move with the present, and find new ways to live—even after loss.

- **GG reminds us that love, once given, never disappears.**

- **The Cat Squad teaches us that life continues, even after painful endings.**

- **And every cat, in their own way, shows us that attachment isn't about holding on—it's about being fully present in the moment.**

So when life asks you to let go, remember: Love remains, change is inevitable, and moving forward doesn't mean forgetting—it just means making space for what comes next.

Chapter 11: My Daughter, The Partner in Crime & The Husband

"The Universe provides help in the most unexpected places. Sometimes, in the form of a fierce protector armed with a jug of water."

Managing the Cat Squad would have been significantly more challenging without my two unexpected allies: my daughter and The Husband. While the cats demand attention, food, protection, and sometimes crisis management, these two have been my steadfast support system, stepping up in ways I never expected.

The Partner in Crime—My Daughter, The Right-Hand Cat Guardian

My daughter is right beside me during feeding time. She instinctively knows what's needed before I even ask—whether it's grabbing an extra bowl, keeping an eye on a newcomer, or handing me the stick when a territorial dog needs discouragement.

She's my second pair of hands. When a new cat joins unexpectedly, she ensures they're fed without delay.

She's the tactical assistant. If I need to separate a fight, she's already armed with what's necessary—be it food, distraction, or a well-placed deterrent.

She makes it all more fun. Managing a feline kingdom isn't always easy but having someone to share the absurdity and joy makes all the difference.

Human Takeaway: When you have a mission, find the right people to share it with. Support doesn't always come in the form of grand gestures—sometimes, it's just showing up consistently.

The Husband: From Cat Sceptic to Fierce Protector

The Husband's journey with the Cat Squad is perhaps the greatest transformation of them all. Once upon a time, he was indifferent—at best—toward cats. And then GG arrived.

Something about her tiny, fearless nature melted his resistance. Maybe it was her way of playfully frolicking around us, or how she demanded attention without apology. But slowly, he began to change. And now? He is the cats' ultimate protector.

The Ever-Vigilant Guardian: He's the one reminding me when the food supply is running low and which cat has been lurking around, waiting to be fed.

The Summoner of Attention: He's the one saying, "There's a cat at the door!" even before I've noticed.

The Water God: When dogs need to be discouraged from pestering the cats, The Husband appears water jug in hand, ready to rain down justice.

But his true transformation became evident after GG's passing. He was right with me when we took her to the vet. He was right with me when my heart broke and I had to bury her. He's the one who dug her grave and wrapped her in my old sweater to keep her warm. And he was furious. He swore vengeance on the dogs that attacked her. His grief, while misguided in its call for retribution, came from a place of deep love and helplessness.

It was tough explaining to him that this is simply how nature unfolds. That as much as we want to protect them, we can't control everything.

Yet, through this, I realized something profound: When your heart is in the right place, and your intentions are true, the Universe sends help in ways you never expect.

Human Takeaway: Even the most unexpected allies can become your greatest support system. People may not start out where you are, but when they care, they show up.

Final Thoughts: Finding Support in Unexpected Places

I never imagined that the people closest to me would become so deeply intertwined in this cat-filled journey. My daughter, always beside me, anticipating what's needed. The Husband, once a cat sceptic, now a sworn feline protector. Their presence, in small and big ways, has made managing the Cat Squad not just easier, but infinitely more meaningful.

- **My daughter reminds me that shared missions make any challenge easier.**
- **The Husband teaches me that transformation happens in unexpected ways.**

- **And the Universe, in its own way, always provides the right support—when the heart is in the right place.**

Chapter 12: Managing the Cat Squad—Trial, Error & a Dash of Strategy

"Adaptability isn't just a skill—it's survival. Whether managing cats or life, those who adjust thrive."

Managing the Cat Squad has been a journey of trial and error. I have been scratched, bitten, hissed at, and ignored. But over time, I've developed a rhythm—a way to communicate with them, anticipate their needs, and manage their ever-evolving dynamics.

This didn't happen overnight. It took patience, observation, and a whole lot of improvisation. But one thing has become clear: if you're willing to put in the effort, the cats will meet you halfway.

From Chaos to Coordination: Creating a Meal-Time System

At first, feeding time was a battlefield. Swatting, hissing, and dramatic stand-offs were the norm, as if every cat believed that unless they fought for their food, they wouldn't be fed.

Consistency Creates Trust. Over time, they learned that everyone would be fed—there's no scarcity here.

Timing is Everything. They now enter one after the other, minimizing the time they have to share space.

Strategic Bowl Placement Prevents Cat Wars. When more than one cat arrives at the same time, I have multiple bowls placed at strategic distances—far enough to prevent swatting but close enough for peaceful coexistence.

Meal times are mostly peaceful now. (I hope I haven't spoken too soon!) But if there's one thing I've learned from this squad, it's to always expect the unexpected.

The Ever-Growing Cat Squad

Currently, the regulars are Batman, Daisy, Vivian, Maple, Chairman Mao, and Casper. They've established their routines, their pecking order (with some disputes, of course), and an unspoken understanding of how this system works.

But I know this is just the beginning.

Word is spreading. More cats may join the mix, and I'm honestly looking forward to it.

The kittens are coming. Daisy, Maple, and Vivian have had their litters, and sooner or later, they too will make their presence felt.

Final Thoughts: Leadership, Adaptability & The Art of Herding Cats

Managing this squad has taught me more about adaptability, patience, and leadership than any formal training ever could.

- **Consistency builds trust. Whether with cats or people, reliable actions create security.**

- **Anticipation prevents conflict. If you can foresee potential issues, you can prevent chaos before it happens.**

- **When you lead with care, they respond. Cats may be independent, but they recognize effort. Show up, and they'll meet you halfway.**

I may not have planned for this growing feline kingdom, but now that I'm here? I wouldn't have it any other way.

Chapter 13: What My Feline Overlords Taught Me About Life

"Live with confidence. Set boundaries. Trust your instincts. And always make time for a nap in the sun."

If someone had told me years ago that I would be running an ever-growing feline kingdom, complete with hierarchies, territorial battles, unexpected alliances, and diplomatic negotiations over food bowls, I would have laughed. Yet, here we are.

What started with a single meowing kitten under a bike has turned into a full-blown life experiment in leadership, boundaries, relationships, and mindfulness. Each cat—whether through headbutts, slaps, strategic retreats, or sheer indifference—has left me with lessons that extend far beyond the back door.

Key Lessons from My Feline Overlords

Leadership isn't about control—it's about presence. Batman never chases authority. He simply exists with confidence and certainty, and the others follow. True leadership is about embodying trust and stability rather than demanding compliance.

Boundaries are non-negotiable. Daisy reminds me daily that you don't have to explain, justify, or soften your limits. A well-placed hiss (or in human terms, a firm "no") is enough.

Trust is earned, not demanded. Vivian took months to come close, but when she did, it was on her terms. Respect people's timelines, and they'll show up when they're ready.

Rejection is not personal. Batman gets slapped regularly by Daisy, Maple, and Chairman Mao. Does he sulk? No. He moves on, fully intact. We should all learn to handle rejection with such grace.

Adaptability is survival. Managing this squad has taught me that rigid expectations lead to frustration, but flexibility leads to peace. Plans will change. Cats will fight. Kittens will appear out of nowhere. Adjust, and keep going.

Loss is inevitable, but love remains. GG was the beginning of it all, and even though she's gone, her presence lingers. Love doesn't disappear; it simply changes form.

The Universe provides help in unexpected ways. Whether through my daughter's unwavering support, or The Husband's unexpected transformation into The Water God, I've learned that when you're aligned with purpose, the right people (and cats) will show up.

Final Thoughts: How to Live Like a Cat

If there's one takeaway from this entire experience, it's that cats have life figured out. They don't overthink, they don't cling to the past, and they don't waste energy on things that don't matter. They set boundaries unapologetically, demand love without hesitation, and walk away from situations that don't serve them.

- **Lead with confidence, not control.**

- **Set boundaries without guilt.**

- **Trust takes time—respect the process.**

- **Rejection isn't failure—move on with dignity.**

- **Stay adaptable, because life will change.**

- **Love fiercely, but don't cling.**

- **And above all—enjoy the warmth of the sun, take the nap, and never forget that you deserve to be fed first.**

This book may be about cats, but the wisdom? It's for all of us.

End Credits: No Cats Were Harmed (But Many Egos Were Bruised)

Because in this kingdom, drama is inevitable, hierarchy is fluid, and only the food bowl is sacred. No tails were stepped on during the making of this book... intentionally.

Executive Producers

- **GG** – For walking in, changing everything, and walking out like a legend.

- **Batman** – For maintaining silent authority while doing absolutely nothing.

- **Vivian** – For insisting on mood lighting and emotional depth in every chapter.

Writers' Room (They Dictated, I Just Typed)

- **Chairman Mao** – Meowed every scene into existence. Loudly.

- **Daisy** – Provided suspicious glances and sassy side commentary.

- **Smokey** – Only showed up for the conflict scenes. Nailed it.

Stunt Coordination

- **Maple** – For acrobatic bowl-dodging and Oscar-worthy drama yowls.

- **Mittens** – Specializing in disappearing acts and trust fall experiments.

Spiritual Consultant

- **Ginger** – For brief but meaningful cameos and universal wisdom. Rumoured to have arrived via wormhole. Cannot confirm.

Security & Crowd Control

- **Casper the Dog** – For taking his self-appointed job way too seriously. Also nominated for "Most Likely to Start Barking After It's Over."

Humans (AKA Staff)

- **The Author** – Head Butler, Mealtime Mediator, and Student of Paw-losophy.

- **The Daughter** – Tactical Support, Stick-Wielding Sidekick & Cat Whisperer-in-Training.

- **The Husband** – Hydration Officer, Reformed Sceptic, and Water Jug Wielder of Justice.

Special Mentions

- The ever-rotating collection of disposable bowls — some cracked from enthusiastic chewing, others stolen by jealous dogs with identity crises.

- The multiple street corners where everyone pees to assert dominance like furry warlords.

- The unnamed lizard who briefly joined the squad and regretted it.

- The neighbourhood stray dogs who came, saw, and promptly left — not because they weren't tough, but because they understood: this level of chaos requires emotional resilience.

Gone But Not Forgotten

Legend of the Lane

GG – The Original Gangsta Girl

She came meowing from under a bike, walked into our hearts, and never let go.

Tiny body, giant spirit, master of silent boundaries and big lessons.

She taught us how to love fiercely, set limits gracefully, and accept the inevitable with courage.

She didn't just start the Cat Squad — she founded a feline empire.

We still hear her echoes in the evening breeze, feel her presence in the quiet corners, and know she's watching us from somewhere with unlimited wet food and zero dogs.

Outtakes & Bloopers

Because when you work with cats, perfection is a myth and chaos is the aesthetic. There are no retakes in cat parenting — just new episodes.

- **Batman** once walked straight into a wall because he was staring down a rival mid-strut. Still acted like it was intentional.

- **Vivian** once didn't like the way Maple looked at her and responded with the loudest, filthiest yowl this side of the galaxy. Maple didn't blink. Drama: 10/10. Resolution: still pending.

- **Daisy** was once caught licking a dog biscuit. Immediately hissed at it like it seduced her.

- **Chairman Mao** launched a protest mid-meal when served chicken instead of fish. Her meow echoed for a full three minutes.

- **Smokey** tried to jump the boundary wall to impress Vivian, missed, and pretended to clean his paw to save face.

- **Maple** once screamed because her own tail  brushed her leg. Twice.

- **Mittens** was once startled by a leaf and disappeared for two days. The leaf was later interrogated and cleared of all charges.

- **Casper** got into a turf war with his reflection in a steel bowl. The reflection won.

- **The Husband** once stood guard with the water jug… heroically facing the wrong alley while the cats were ambushed from behind. He later blamed "misleading paw signals."

- **The Author** once sprinted to rescue Smokey from a dog... only to discover it was a pile of trash bags shaped exactly like Smokey.

- **The Daughter** invented the "double-stick defence formation" — only to drop both sticks mid-charge when a cat sneezed unexpectedly.

Until the Next Meow...